DARE TO DREAM AGAIN!

STUDY GUIDE

Dare To Dream Again!

Study Guide

It's Never Too Late For a New Beginning

By

Miranda Burnette

Keys to Success Publishing, LLC

Atlanta, GA

Unless otherwise indicated, all Scripture quotations are taken from the *King James Version* (KJV) of the Bible.

Scripture quotations marked (AMPC) are taken from the *Amplified Bible Classic Edition.*

Scripture quotations marked (NIV) are taken from the *Holy Bible, New International Version.*

Scripture quotations marked (MSG) are taken from the *Message Bible.*

Scripture quotations marked (NKJV) are taken from the *New King James Version of the Bible.*

Scripture quotations marked (NLT) are taken from the *Holy Bible, New Living Translation.*

Scripture quotations marked (NASB) are taken from the *New American Standard Bible.*

Dare To Dream Again: Study Guide – It's Never too Late For a New Beginning

ISBN: 978-0692063392

P. O. Box 314
Clarkdale, GA 30111

www.mirandaburnetteministries.org

Keys to Success Publishing
Atlanta, GA 30127

Cover Design by Jackie Moore

TABLE OF CONTENTS

HOW TO USE THIS STUDY

Whether you are leading a small group, teaching a class, or studying on your own, this study guide is designed for you to get a deeper understanding of God's Word, the Bible. In addition, this study guide will reinforce the principles taught in my book, *Dare to Dream Again.* Here is how it works.

Step 1: Before you begin, please read the corresponding chapter in the book, *Dare to Dream Again.*

Step 2: Read the *Lesson Summary,* the first section in this study guide.

Step 3: Answer the *Study Questions* in the study guide by referring to the material in the book, *Dare to Dream Again,* the *Lesson Summary,* or the *Bible.*

Step 4: Once you have finished answering the questions in each lesson, turn to the *Answer Key* provided at the back of the study guide to check your answers.

Step 5: Answer the *Discussion Questions.* There are no right or wrong answers.

Step 6: Complete the *Life Application* Activity.

Step 7: Read and meditate on the list of *Scriptures* located at the end of each lesson. If you desire, you may also, memorize some of the scripture verses. This is an important step because those scripture verses are the basis of the teaching in each lesson.

Step 8: Read the list of *Inspirational Quotes* located at the end of each lesson.

Materials Needed: Bible, Study Guide, the book, *Dare to Dream Again* and a writing utensil.

INTRODUCTION

Have you ever dreamed of winning something, being something, or starting something? Maybe you have dreamed of starting your own business, earning a degree, becoming a professional athlete, artist, or musician.

We are born dreamers! When a person gets older, when they stop dreaming, when they've lost the vision, life just isn't the same. When you stop dreaming, it seems as if a part of you is missing. Nothing else seems to fulfill you as much as the desire to realize or accomplish your dream.

God has a specific plan designed for each of our lives. Nevertheless, it is our responsibility to stay on the path to our dream. We must hold on to the dream, cooperate with God, and fulfill the plan He has for our lives.

If you have lost sight of your dream, and given up on your dream, it is time to dream again! At one time in your life, you may have had a dream God had placed in your heart. You might have pursued that dream with all you had within you. You felt like you had all of the passion and determination you needed to accomplish that dream. However, as time passed, it seemed as though this wonderful dream was taking forever to manifest in your life.

When we are pursuing our dreams, many times it will take longer than we expected, cost more than we thought it would, and require a lot more hard work than we could ever imagine. In addition, the people who you expected to support you will not support you at all. On the other hand, the people you did not expect to support you will support you.

As you pursue your dream, think about this: Are you pursuing your own plan and expecting or even asking God to bless it? When we are pursuing our dreams, we must walk in step with God. We can't get ahead of God, nor can we lag behind Him. We have to be in agreement with Him. We have to first, do what He leads or call us to do. We have to do it when He tells us to do it, and we have to do it His way.

When God places a dream in your heart, it doesn't happen overnight. It doesn't just appear. We have to do something. We have to put forth some effort to realize our dreams. We have to add corresponding action to our faith.

Success is a process. What we become in the process is far more important than the dream itself. The kind of person you become, the character you build, the courage you develop, and how strong your faith becomes is something that will benefit you throughout your lifetime and in every area of your life.

Success is not a destination; it is a journey. It takes time and small steps of consistent effort to reach our goals and make our dreams come true. The good news about pursuing our dreams is, God is right there to help us every step of the way.

One thing we have to remember though is this: Do not run off and leave God behind. We have to realize that with God all things are possible (Matthews 19:26), and we can do all things through Christ who gives us the strength and power (Philippians 4:13). Without God, we can do nothing (John 15:5).

Sometimes working on our dreams can get discouraging and appears very overwhelming. It can get to the point where you just want to throw up your hands and say, "I give up, I just can't do this anymore, I am too old for this, or this is just too much for me." However, I am here to tell you today, "Don't give up!" It is never too late to dream again.

This time around don't leave God out of the picture. Also, make sure your dream is in line with God's will and plan for your life. God is not obligated to anoint anything He does not initiate. Whatever God orders, He pays for.

Furthermore, if He gives you the dream or vision, He will also provide the provision. God gives us the grace to do whatever He places in our hearts and is His will for our lives. So depend on and trust God with all of your heart and *Dare to Dream Again!*

You may have dreams that have been shattered, but get back into the race and dream again. It is never too late with God. You are not too old. You did not mess up so badly that God can't fix it. You have what it takes. You have hope. You can do it!

With God on your side, you can't fail. God is a God of impossibilities. Starting all over might not be easy, but with God's help, you can win! God is your strength. He is everything you need.

To climb the ladder of success, we have to persevere. We have to keep moving. We have to press on. We have to ignore criticism and negativity.

When you are pursuing your dream, many days it will be only you and God. You may get lonely sometimes. Many things may happen that you will not understand, but hold on and keep moving forward keeping your eyes on the prize of your dream.

Life has a way of pushing our dreams down. We have so many responsibilities and we can become so busy and preoccupied that we give up on our dreams and forget about them.

It is easy to get sidetracked and lose your dream. You may have backed off the dream God has given you. You may have lost your dream, but get back on course and dream again. Fulfill the dream God has given you and be all God created you to be. It's not too late to start living your dream. *It's never too late to dream again!*

As you work through this study guide, it is my sincere prayer that you will pick up the shattered pieces of your dream and rekindle the passion you once had and *Dare to Dream Again!* Once you start dreaming again, this time, don't let anyone or anything stop you from living your dream! Hold on to your dream and don't let it go!

LESSON 1

THE GOD OF A SECOND CHANCE

LESSON SUMMARY

We serve a God of a second chance. God is merciful and full of love and compassion. God also continually gives us supernatural favor and grace.

What are setbacks? Setbacks are life interruptions. A setback is something that causes delay or stops progress. There are several types of setbacks. A divorce or someone walking out of your life can be a setback. Other types of setbacks are; the death of a loved one, the loss of a job, a dream shattered, a health issue, or a failed business.

An example of someone experiencing a setback in the Bible is Job. Job was the richest man in the East, but he lost everything. God helped Job come back from a setback. When you fall down, get back up. Falling down is a part of life. Falling down is also a part of success. We learn to walk by falling, just as a baby does. Getting back up is not easy. God will not give up on you so don't give up on yourself.

We all make mistakes in different areas of our lives such as, in our finances, our careers, our parenting, our marriages, and in our business deals. Our failures can leave us feeling that God could never use us again. God gives second chances when we make mistakes, and we can began again.

If God gives second chances, we should also give second chances to others. We must imitate God by forgiving and giving the people in our lives second chances. God wants you to give others a second chance

We have to remember that love is patient, loves keeps no record of the wrong done to it, love always hopes, love always perseveres, and love gives a second chance.

1

The struggles in life are necessary for our growth and development. Flight and life are in the struggle.

Without challenges and struggles, we would never grow, and reach our fullest potential. If you want to see success in achieving your dreams, you must work through difficulties and 'Dare to Dream Again.'

STUDY QUESTIONS

1. Name four characteristics of God that describes Him as a God of a second chance.

_____

_____

_____

2. What does the statement, "You and God are a majority" mean?

_____

_____

_____

3. What are setbacks?

_____

_____

_____

4. Name five examples of a setback.

_____

_____

_____

_____

_____

5. Name a Bible Character who had a setback that caused him to lose everything.

_____

DARE TO DREAM AGAIN

DISCUSSION QUESTIONS

1. Have you ever experienced a setback in your own life? If so, explain.

   _____

   _____

   _____

2. When you experience setbacks, how do you handle them?

   _____

   _____

   _____

3. Is there someone in your life you have felt like giving up on? If so, why?

   _____

   _____

   _____

4. What are some ways you have given others in your life a second chance?

   _____

   _____

5. What strategies do you use to work through challenges in order to achieve success?

   _____

   _____

LIFE APPLICATION

What are steps you can take to comeback from a setback? Using the chart on the following page, write the steps and how you plan to achieve each step.

"Just like springtime is a fresh new beginning after the long cold winter, God also gives us second chances...a fresh start for another try to become a new you... Trust and have faith, and let Him fill you with His love and make you new again."

- Karen Kostyla

Coming Back From A Setback

Step 1

Step 2

Step 3

Step 4

SCRIPTURES

For His anger is but for a moment, but His favor is for a lifetime or in His favor is life. Weeping may endure for a night, but joy comes in the morning.

Psalm 30:5 (AMPC)

Then he told this parable: "A man had a fig tree growing in his vineyard, and he went to look for fruit on it but did not find any.

So he said to the man who took care of the vineyard, 'For three years now I've been coming to look for fruit on this fig tree and haven't found any. Cut it down! Why should it use up the soil?'

"'Sir,' the man replied, 'leave it alone for one more year, and I'll dig around it and fertilize it.

If it bears fruit next year, fine! If not, then cut it down.'"

Luke 13:6-9 (NIV)

The Lord is merciful and gracious, slow to anger and abounding in steadfast love.

Psalm 103: 8 (ESV)

For though the righteous fall seven times, they rise again, but the wicked stumble when calamity strikes.

Proverbs 24:16 (NIV)

If you faint in the day of adversity, Your strength is small.

Proverbs 24:10(NKJV)

INSPIRATIONAL QUOTES

"Just like springtime is a fresh new beginning after the long cold winter, God also gives us second chances…a fresh start for another try to become a new you… Trust and have faith, and let Him fill you with His love and make you new again…"

__Karen Kostyla

"The greatest power in life is not never falling, but in rising every time you fall."

__Nelson Mandela

"You may not be responsible for being knocked down, but you are responsible for getting back up!"

__ Jesse Jackson

"It's not whether you get knocked down; It's whether you get up again."

__Vince Lombardi

"Our greatest weakness lies in giving up. The most certain way to succeed is always to try just one more time.

__ Thomas Edison

"Any day that we don't give up puts us one day closer to success."

__ Joyce Meyer

"It's never too late to be what you might have been."

__George Eliot

The Land of Begin Again

"I wish that there were some wonderful place called the land of Begin Again, where all our mistakes and all our heartaches and all our poor selfish grief…Could be dropped like a shabby old coat at the door and never be put on again. I wish that

there were some wonderful place called The Land of Begin Again."

__Louisa Tarkington

"We go through life with a series of God-ordained opportunities, brilliantly disguised as challenges."

__Charles Udall

"The conquering of adversity produces strength of character, forges self-confidence, engenders self-respect, and assures success in righteous endeavor."

__Richard G. Scott

"Every crucial experience can be regarded either as a setback, or the start of a wonderful new adventure, it depends on your perspective!"

__ Mary Roberts Rinehart

"Good timber does not grow with ease; the stronger the wind, the stronger the trees."

__ J. Willard Marriott

"Having a dream, living that dream, losing that dream, dreaming again and then having that dream come true again is one of the greatest feelings ever because I'm stronger."

__Aaron Carter

"When individuals rise above their circumstances and use problems to push them to become more, they grasp greatness."

__ Nelson Mandela

LESSON 2

DARE TO DREAM AGAIN

LESSON SUMMARY

As adults, we sometimes lose our faith and hope to dream because others don't believe in our dreams or even in us. When God gives us a dream, He also gives us faith to believe for and accomplish that dream. God will not give someone else faith for *your* dream. Sometimes life gets in the way of our dreams. Responsibilities increase, and our passion and creativity are lost.

People stop dreaming for various reasons. The fear of failure is one reason. The fear of failure is the apprehension that you *will never* reach your goal. Fear will paralyze you and you will become stuck in a rut. Sometimes you have to do it afraid. Most people who are successful and make their dreams come true have experienced many failures. Thomas Edison, Henry Ford, Walt Disney, Reggie Jackson, Michael Jordan, and Albert Einstein have all experienced failures on their journey to success, but each one became a success.

The fear of success is another reason many people stop dreaming. The fear of success is being afraid that you *will* reach your goal. The fear of success can hold you back from God's best for your life. When fear attacks us, we can use our spiritual weapons of prayer, faith, and the Word of God to win the war over fear in our lives.

Staying in the comfort zone is another reason people stop dreaming. A comfort zone is a place we settle into that is familiar, low stress, and has few or no challenges. The comfort zone consists of the known, the accepted, and the expected. Moving out of the comfort zone can be very frightening to some people.

Feeling unworthy of success can also stop people from dreaming. An acceptance of yourself that you are worthy has to be achieved first, before you believe of yourself that others will accept you as well. People who don't feel worthy of success, do not believe in themselves. Believe in yourself

Associating with the wrong people will stop you from dreaming. Surround yourself with winners. We need to be aware of the company we keep because we become like those we associate with. We need to spend time with positive people.

Procrastination will stop most people from dreaming. Procrastination means to put off habitually the doing of something that should be done. Procrastination is a dream thief.

Thinking you are too old will stop you from dreaming. You are never too old to have goals. Thinking you are too old will stop you from ever living your dreams. It is all in how you look at it.

If you have allowed any of these things to become a roadblock between you and your dream, be determined to overcome those barriers and dream again. It is time to dream again! Keep dreaming until your dream becomes a reality in your life.

STUDY QUESTIONS

1. Why do adults sometimes lose faith and hope to dream?

    _____
    _____

2. When God gives us a dream, what else does He give us with it?

    _____
    _____
    _____

3. What sometimes gets in the way of our dreams?

    _____
    _____

4. What are seven reasons people stop dreaming?

    _____
    _____
    _____
    _____
    _____
    _____
    _____

5. What is the fear of failure?

    _____
    _____
    _____

DISCUSSION QUESTION

1. Have you ever had a dream that you gave up on it? If you did, why did you give up on your dream?

   _____

   _____

   _____

2. What do you believe caused you to give up on your dream?

   _____

   _____

3. What have you heard or read in this lesson that sparked your passion and inspired you to dream again?

   _____

   _____

4. How do you plan to avoid the same mistakes again when you are tempted to give up on your dream?

   _____

   _____

   _____

5. What would you tell someone you know who is about to give up on his or her dream?

   _____

   _____

   _____

   _____

LIFE APPLICATION

What is your dream or your new dream? Write it in the center of the oval shape on the graphic organizer on the following page. In the six remaining squares, write down six reasons why you are so passionate about this dream and why it means so much to you.

"Don't be afraid to get back up, to try again, to love again, to live again, and to dream again."

- Author Unknown

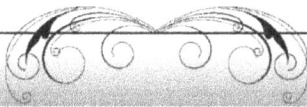

It's Time To Dream Again!

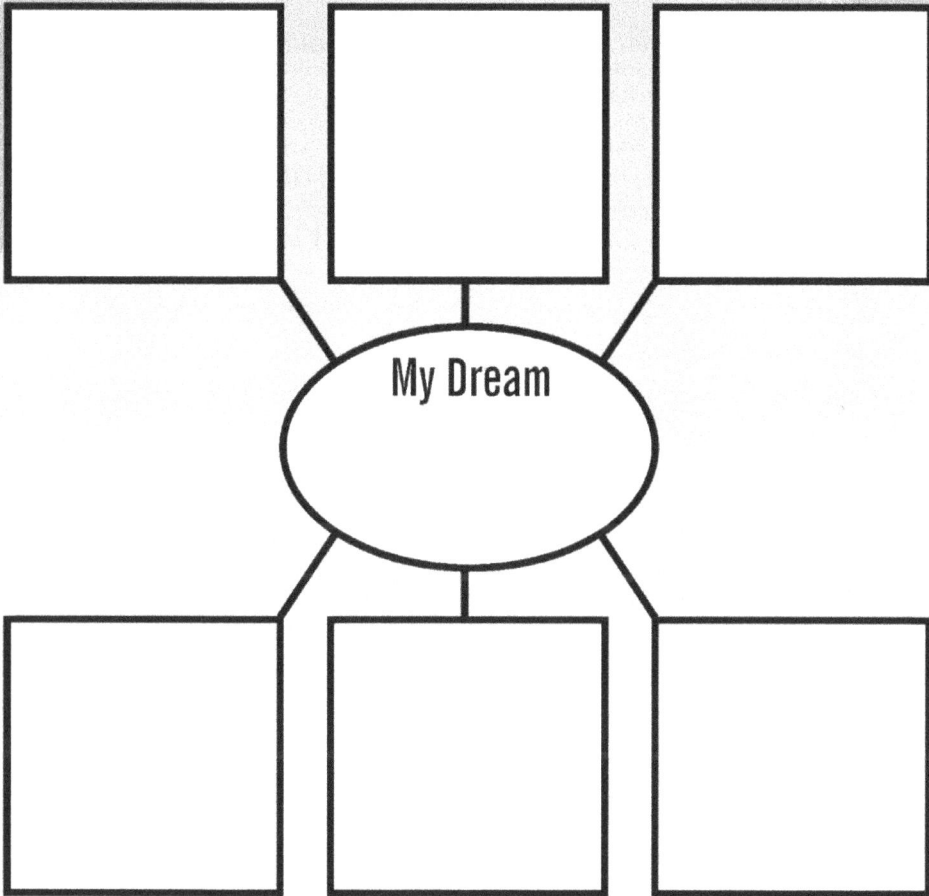

My Dream

SCRIPTURES

For God has not given us a spirit of fear, but of power and of love and of a sound mind.

2 Timothy 1:7 (NKJV)

Do not be misled: "Bad company corrupts good character."

1 Corinthians 15:33 (NIV)

INSPIRATIONAL QUOTES

"Don't be afraid to get back up, to try again, to love again, to live again, and to dream again."

__Author Unknown

"Do what you fear and your fear will die."

__Ralph Waldo Emerson

Courage is acting in spite of fear."

__Howard W. Hunter

"I failed my way to success."

__Thomas Edison

"Failure is only the opportunity to begin again, this time more intelligently."

__Henry Ford

"All the adversity I've had in my life, all my troubles and obstacles, have strengthened me... You may not realize it when it happens, but a kick in the teeth may be the best thing in the world for you."

__Walt Disney

"I feel that the most important requirement in success is learning to overcome failure. You must learn to tolerate it, but never accept it."

__Reggie Jackson

"I've missed more than 9,000 shots in my career. I've lost almost 300 games. Twenty-six times, I've been trusted to take the game winning shot and missed. I've failed over and over and over again in my life, and that is why I succeed."

__Michael Jordan

19

"Failure is success in progress."

__Albert Einstein

"We will sometimes have defeats in life but you can have defeats without being defeated, you can fail without being a failure. Winners see failure and defeats as merely part of the process to get to win."

__ Maya Angelou

"The greatest mistake we make is living in constant fear that we will make one."

__ John Maxwell

"The only thing we have to fear is fear itself."

__ Franklin D. Roosevelt

"If you do what you've always done, you'll get what you've always gotten."

__Tony Robbins

"If you want to fly with the eagles, you can't continue to scratch with the turkeys."

__ Zig Ziglar

"Keep away from people who try to belittle your ambitions. Small people always do that, but the really great make you feel that you, too, can become great."

__Mark Twain

"You are as young as your faith, as old as your doubt, as young as your self-confidence, as old as your fear, as young as your hope, and as old as your despair."

__ Paul H. Dunn

LESSON 3

A NEW BEGINNING

LESSON SUMMARY

A New Beginning is a time for a fresh start. It is a chance to do something over, but in a better, more productive way. If we keep holding on to the old, how can we allow God to bring His plan to pass in our lives?

We need to forget the past and make way for the future. God is doing a new thing. The old maybe comfortable or familiar, but if the Lord is finished with the old, His anointing will not continue to be on it. God created us with a need for new beginnings. This is why we have a new beginning every morning. Each day we have an opportunity to begin again. Each day we have an opportunity to start over again.

People hold on to the old for several reasons. Sometimes a person may stay on an old job when God is leading him or her to leave that job for a better job. Some people may experience trials when they step out and then start to think about how things used to be, and desire to go back to the old.

Thinking and talking about the past keeps you trapped in it. Let go of the past, mentally and verbally, and embrace the future. Expect something good to take place. Have an aggressively positive attitude. The word aggressively means making an all-out effort to win or succeed. The beginning of a new year is always a good time to put things in order.

STUDY QUESTIONS

1. A new beginning is a time for what?

    _____

2. What can happen if we keep holding on to the old?

    _____

    _____

3. How can we make way for the future?

    _____

    _____

4. What happens to something in our lives when God is finished with it?

    _____

    _____

5. According to Lamentations 3:22-23 (AMPC), what is new every morning?

    _____

    _____

DISCUSSION QUESTIONS

1. Can you think of a time in your life when you were hanging on to something old, and you believed God was telling you to let it go?

   _____

   _____

   _____

2. Name three examples of someone hanging on to old things.

   _____

   _____

3. How can thinking and talking about the past keep you trapped in it?

   _____

   _____

4. How can a person have an aggressively positive attitude?

   _____

   _____

5. What are two examples of how to start the year with a fresh start?

   _____

   _____

LIFE APPLICATION

Use the flow chart on the following page to describe something old you have been holding on to in the first rectangle shape. In the second rectangle shape, describe something new you would like to replace the old with in your life. In the last rectangle shape, list three actions you can take to help make something new happen.

"*Every day is a new beginning, treat it that way. Stay away from what might have been, and look at what can be.*"

– Marsha Petrie Sue

Action Plan

Old Thing

New Thing

Take Action

SCRIPTURES

Forget the former things; do not dwell on the past. See, I am doing a new thing! Now it springs up; do you not perceive it? I am making a way in the desert and streams in the wasteland.

Isaiah 43:18-19 (NIV)

It is because of the Lord's mercy and loving-kindness that we are not consumed, because His [tender] compassions fail not. They are new every morning; great and abundant is Your stability and faithfulness.

Lamentations 3:22-23 (AMPC)

And He Who is seated on the throne said, See! I make all things new. Also He said, Record this, for these sayings are faithful (accurate, incorruptible, and trustworthy) and true (genuine).

Revelations 21:5 (AMPC)

For behold, I create new heavens and a new earth. And the former things shall not be remembered or come into mind.

Isaiah 65:17 (AMPC)

Behold, the days are coming, says the Lord, when I will make a new covenant with the house of Israel and with the house of Judah.

Jeremiah 31:31 (AMPC)

Therefore if any person is [ingrafted] in Christ (the Messiah) he is a new creation (a new creature altogether); the old [previous moral and spiritual condition] has passed away. Behold, the fresh and new has come!

2 Corinthians 5:17 (AMPC)

INSPIRATIONAL QUOTES

"Every day is a new beginning, treat it that way. Stay away from what might have been, and look at what can be."

__Marsha Petrie Sue

"For it matters not how small the beginning may seem to be: what is once done well is done forever."

__ Henry David Thoreau

"Never let your small beginnings make you small-minded. Have vision beyond your circumstances."

__Brendon Burchard

"There is safety in small beginnings and there is unlimited capital in the experience gained by growing."

__Henry Ford

"Great things have small beginnings."

__ Francis Drake

LESSON 4

SMALL BEGINNINGS

LESSON SUMMARY

Do not despise these small beginnings. The word *despise* means dislike, hate, look down on, or undervalue. When we despise something, we are regarding it lightly. Don't despise small things. No one starts at the top. Big things usually start as small things.

Be faithful over little things. If we are faithful in small things, God will be able to trust us with bigger ones. Faithful in the *Greek* means to be reliable and trusted. Faithful according to *Webster* means to be loyal, firmly devoted, worthy of trust, or reliable. A synonym for faithful is constant.

If we don't use or take care of what God gives to us, we will lose it. If we lose the seed that God has given us, we will never see the manifestation of the harvest. If God gives you a blessing in the form of a seed, He will bring it to completion, but we have to cooperate with Him.

Just as God makes each day new, He will make a new you. God will give you a new belief system. God will renew your mind as you read and study His Word and believe it. We have to have a new mindset and we have to have a new attitude. In Christ, you are a new creation.

STUDY QUESTIONS

1. Do not _____small beginnings.

2. What does the word *despise* mean?

   _____

   _____

3. What happens if we are faithful in small things?

   _____

   _____

   _____

4. What does faithful mean in the *Greek* and according to *Webster*?

   _____

   _____

   _____

5. What happens if we don't use or take care of what God gives to us?

   _____

   _____

   _____

DISCUSSION QUESTIONS

1. What does "Small Beginnings" mean?

    _____

    _____

    _____

2. What kind of seeds do you believe God has given to you?

    _____

    _____

    _____

3. How can a person grow just as a seed grows?

    _____

    _____

    _____

4. How can we cooperate with God to bring a blessing He has given to us in seed form to completion in our lives?

    _____

    _____

    _____

5. What does this statement, "God will make a new you" mean?

    _____

    _____

    _____

    _____

LIFE APPLICATION

Use the chart on the following page to write the character qualities you must develop in your life in order to make your dreams a reality. Start at the bottom from the lowest level, *Small Beginnings,* every step of the way on your success journey to the highest level, *A Dream Come True*, as the seed of you dream grows. For example, patience, determination, faith... Remember that from humble beginnings come great things!

"All great things have small beginnings."

- Peter Senge

Stair Steps to Success

A Dream Come True

Small Beginnings

SCRIPTURES

Do not despise these small beginnings, for the Lord rejoices to see the work begin...

Zechariah 4:10 (NLT)

His master replied, 'Well-done, good and faithful servant! You have been faithful with a few things; I will put you in charge of many things. Come and share your master's happiness!'

Matthew 25:21 (NIV)

He that is faithful with little things is faithful with big things also. He that is not honest with little things is not honest with big things.

Luke 16:10 (NLV)

And though your beginning was small, yet your latter end would greatly increase.

Job 8:7 (AMPC)

To everything there is a season, and a time for every matter or purpose under heaven.

Ecclesiastes 3:1 (AMPC)

Therefore, if anyone is in Christ, the new creation has come: The old has gone, the new is here!

2 Corinthians 5:17 (NIV)

Do not lie to one another, since you have put off the old man with his deeds, and have put on the new man who is renewed in knowledge according to the image of Him who created him.

Colossians 3:9-10(NKJV)

INSPIRATIONAL QUOTES

"All great things have small beginnings."

__Peter Senge

"Show me a man who cannot bother to do little things and I'll show you a man who cannot be trusted to do big things."

__Lawrence D. Bell

"Mighty things from small beginnings grow."

__John Dryden

"Big things have small beginnings."

__Michael Fassbender

LESSON 5

PRESSING INTO A NEW BEGINNING

LESSON SUMMARY

Fulfilling your destiny demands letting go of what lies behind. The dreams of the future have no place for the failures of the past. We have to move forward.

Philippians 3: 13-14 tells us to forget what lies behind and strain forward to what lies ahead, and to press on toward the goal to win the prize to which God in Christ Jesus is calling us upward. The word *press* means to exert steady force or pressure. Almost nothing happens worthwhile in our lives without us pressing.

Let go of anything that is holding you back and keeping you from realizing your dreams. We have to be determined to reach our goals. Don't keep trying to hold on to something God is finished with. If you try to hold on to what God is finished with, it will confuse you or frustrate you. Trust God and be led by the Holy Spirit.

If God is finished with something, we need to walk away from it. God could be leading us to walk away from people, situations, places, or a job. Every completion has a new beginning. God wants to bless us with something new.

Wine is made by putting grapes through a press. New wine cannot be put into old wineskins. This means new power cannot be given to someone who is hanging on to old ways. You cannot mix old and new, If you mix old and new, both will be ruined.

With God, all things are possible. Times get tough sometimes. We have to press through hard times and trials. We have to keep on pressing when we want to give up.

STUDY QUESTIONS

1. What is one thing that needs to happen before we can fulfill our destiny?

   _____

   _____

2. Complete the following statement, "The dreams of the future have no place

   for _____."

3. What does Philippians 3:13-14 tell us to forget?

   _____

   _____

4. What does the word *press* mean?

   _____

   _____

5. What do we have to be in order to reach our goals?

   _____

   _____

DISCUSSION QUESTIONS

1. Why doesn't the dreams of the future have no place for the past?

   _____

   _____

2. Why do you think it is so important to press when we are reaching for our goals?

   _____

   _____

3. What are some ways we can be determined to reach our goals?

   _____

   _____

4. What are somethings that can hold you back or keep you from realizing your dreams?

   _____

   _____

5. How can we identify something in our lives that God is finished with?

   _____

   _____

LIFE APPLICATION

Use the ladder on the following page to label each rung to represent obstacles or challenges you must press through to reach your goal as you climb the success ladder.

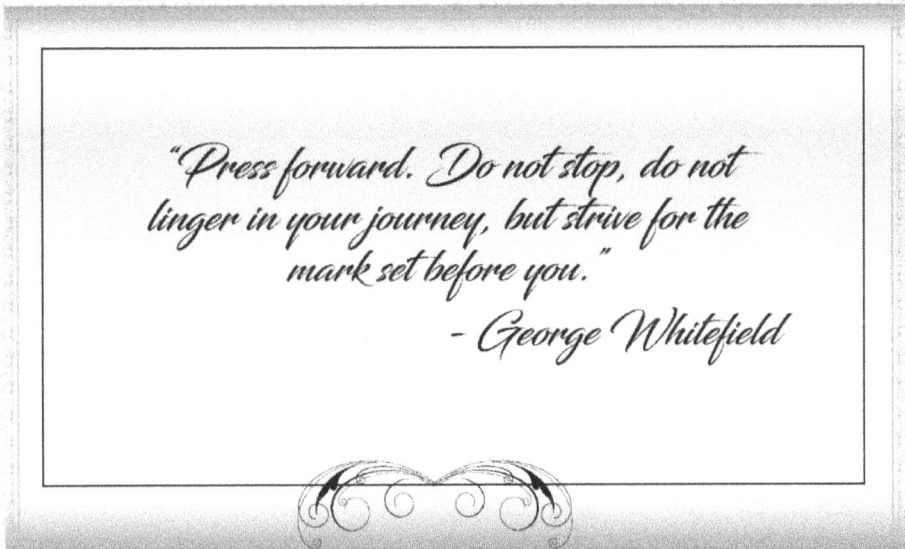

"Press forward. Do not stop, do not linger in your journey, but strive for the mark set before you."

- George Whitefield

My Goals

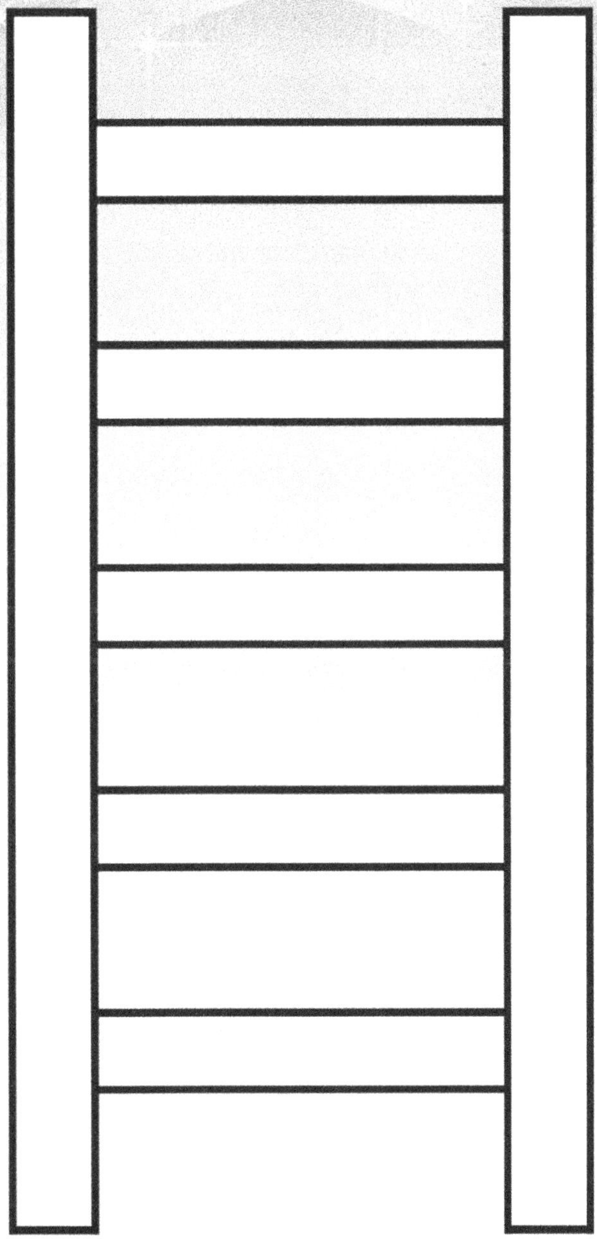

SCRIPTURES

I do not consider, brethren, that I have captured and made it my own [yet]; but one thing I do [it is my one aspiration]; forgetting what lies behind and straining forward to what lies ahead.

I press on toward the goal to win the [supreme and heavenly] prize to which God in Christ Jesus is calling us upward.

Philippians 3:13-14 (AMPC)

And no one pours new wine into old wineskins; if he does, the fresh wine will burst the skins and it will be spilled and the skins will be ruined (destroyed).

Luke 5:37 (AMPC)

And a certain woman, which had an issue of blood twelve years, And had suffered many things of many physicians, and had spent all that she had, and was nothing bettered, but rather grew worse, When she had heard of Jesus, came in the press behind, and touched his garment.

Mark 5:25 – 27 (KJV)

INSPIRATIONAL QUOTES

"Press forward. Do not stop, do not linger in your journey, but strive for the mark set before you." __George Whitefield

"Whatever you're facing today, keep going. Keep moving. Keep hoping. Keep pressing on. There is Victory on the other side!"

__Mandy Hale

"Decide today that you won't give up on your dreams and desires. Keep pressing forward, believing that you are anointed and empowered."

Anonymous

LESSON 6

DON'T LOOK BACK

LESSON SUMMARY

Look straight ahead; don't look back. Looking back can slow you down in your Christian walk. Looking back can hinder your progress when you are working on your dream. Looking back can keep you from doing what God is calling you to do. Looking back can keep you from reaching your goals and realizing your dreams. Looking back can cause you to lose your focus, distract you, and get you off track.

Proverbs 4:25 (ESV) says, "Let your eyes look directly forward, and your gaze be straight before you."

Stay focused on the vision God has given to you. Keep allowing God to prepare you for what He has called you to do. We have to lay aside every weight such as sin, uncontrolled affection, worries, and concerns.

Looking back can be extremely dangerous to a person's success. Looking back can do the following things to destroy your success: hold you back, bring defeat, and paralyze your actions to affect your future. Looking back at defeat will get you down and you will become discouraged. Keep looking forward to the finished line to success.

When you look back, you see all of your past mistakes, faults, and failures. Don't focus on what you *did not* accomplish, but focus on what you *can* accomplish. God can make miracles out of mistakes.

STUDY QUESTIONS

1. Name five problems that can be caused by constantly looking back.

   _____

   _____

   _____

   _____

2. What does proverbs 4:25 (ESV) tell us to do that can prevent us from looking back?

   _____

   _____

3. What are three ways looking back can be extremely dangerous to a person's success?

   _____

   _____

4. What can be seen when you look back?

   _____

   _____

5. God can make _____ out of mistakes.
   a. Mountains
   b. Miracles
   c. Success

DISCUSSION QUESTIONS

1. In what situation in your life do you need to heed God's instruction not to look back?

   _____

   _____

   _____

2. Why is it so vital not to look back when you are trying to reach your goals?

   _____

   _____

3. Why do you think people often look back when they are trying to make their dreams a reality?

   _____

   _____

   _____

4. Why is focus so important?

   _____

   _____

   _____

5. Have you ever experienced God turning a *mistake* you made into a *miracle* in your own life? Explain.

   _____

   _____

   _____

LIFE APPLICATION

Use the chart on the following page to write down, on the left side of the chart, things in your past such as, mistakes, faults, and failures, you should forget and leave behind. On the right side of the chart, write down the goals, dreams, and the vision you see ahead in your future that you should focus on.

> "Don't look back! Everyone has failures or mistakes from the past. To have success, you need to learn from your past and value those difficult lessons but do not ever dwell on the past. Simply move forward and make better, more educated decisions from the lessons learned."
>
> – Author Unknown

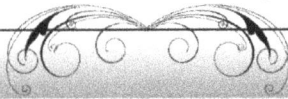

Keep Your Eyes On the Prize

Past   Future

SCRIPTURES

But [Lot's] wife looked back from behind him, and she became a pillar of salt.

Genesis 19:26 (AMPC)

Remember Lot's wife!

Luke 17:32 (AMPC)

Let your eyes look directly forward, and your gaze be straight before you.

Proverbs 4:25 (ESV)

Therefore, since we are encompassed about with such a great cloud of witnesses, let us also lay aside every weight and the sin that so easily entangles us, and let us run with endurance the race that is set before us.

Hebrews 12:1 (MEV)

Don't you realize that in a race everyone runs, but only one person gets the prize? So run to win! All athletes are disciplined in their training. They do it to win a prize that will fade away, but we do it for an eternal prize. So run with purpose in every step. I am not just shadowboxing. I discipline my body like an athlete, training it to do what it should. Otherwise, I fear that after preaching to others I myself might be disqualified.

1 Corinthians 9:24-27 (NLT)

If we confess our sins, he is faithful and just to forgive us our sins and to cleanse us from all unrighteousness.

John 1:9(NKJV)

I, even I, am He Who blots out and cancels your transgressions, for My own sake, and I will not remember your sins.

Isaiah 43:25 (AMPC)

He will again have compassion on us; He will subdue and tread underfoot our iniquities. You will cast all our sins into the depths of the sea.

Micah 7:19 (AMPC)

As far as the east is from the west, so far has He removed our transgressions from us.

Psalm 103:12 (AMPC)

Jesus said to him, no one who puts his hand to the plow and looks back [to the things behind] is fit for the kingdom of God.

Luke 9:62 (AMPC)

INSPIRATIONAL QUOTES

"Don't look back! Everyone has failures or mistakes from the past. To have success, you need to learn from your past and value those difficult lessons but do not ever dwell on the past. Simply move forward and make better, more educated decisions from the lessons learned."

__Author Unknown

"Decide upon your major definite purpose in life and then organize all your activities around it."

__ Brian Tracy

"Every moment wasted looking back, keeps us from moving forward."

__Hillary Clinton

"Once you make the decision to move on, don't look back. Your destiny will never be found in the rear view mirror."

__Mandy Hale

LESSON 7

A NEW WAY OF THINKING

LESSON SUMMARY

Success in any area of your life starts in your mind. Our thoughts determine what kind of life we will have, or whether our dreams will become a reality. If you change your thinking, you will change your life. Your thoughts have a lot to do with where you are right now. Your thoughts will also have a lot to do with where you are going to be in the future. You can't excel beyond your level of thinking. You can't think failure and be a success. You can't think poverty and be prosperous.

According to Romans 12:2, the mind must be renewed by the Word of God. We should think thoughts that are in agreement with God's Word. We should choose thoughts carefully according to where we want to go in life. We must consistently choose right thinking.

Your 'New Way of Thinking' is 'Thinking God's Way.' Think God's thoughts. God's thoughts are His Words, which are in the Bible. To think God's way, you must renew your mind with the Word of God. We need a new way of thinking. The same old way of thinking will produce the same results. The way we think controls our entire life. Our thoughts shape our words, habits, and character. Our thoughts release Gods ability in our lives.

Don't stay trapped in limited thinking. Thinking just because you failed once, it is over for you is limited thinking. Don't think it is over for you and it is too late because you are too old. You are not too old. It is never too late or too early to dream again. God can give you a new dream. Dreaming again starts in your mind. What you put into your mind is what you will get out of it.

To reach your goals, realize your dreams, or accomplish anything in your life, you have to see it before you see it. You see it before you see it, by using your imagination. Whatever you want to build, first, you have to picture it in your imagination before you can build it in the natural. If you want to fulfill God's will for your life, you have to see it on the inside before you can see it on the outside.

STUDY QUESTIONS

1. Where does success start?

   _____

   _____

2. If you change your thinking, you will change your _____.

3. Can you excel above your level of thinking?

   _____

   _____

4. According to Romans 12:2, how must the mind be renewed?

   _____

   _____

   _____

5. What is your new way of thinking?

   _____

   _____

   _____

DISCUSSION QUESTIONS

1. Why do we need a new way of thinking?

    _____

    _____

2. How would you describe limited thinking?

    _____

    _____

3. What are two examples each of "Failure Thinking," and "Success Thinking?"

    _____

    _____

    _____

4. How exactly do you think success starts in the mind?

    _____

    _____

    _____

5. What does "See it before you see it" mean to you?

    _____

    _____

    _____

LIFE APPLICATION

In the graphic organizer on the following page, write down on each cloud, six ways you plan to achieve a "New Way of Thinking" in your life.

"The only way you can sustain a permanent change is to create a new way of thinking, acting, and being.

— Jennifer Hudson

Success Starts in Your Mind

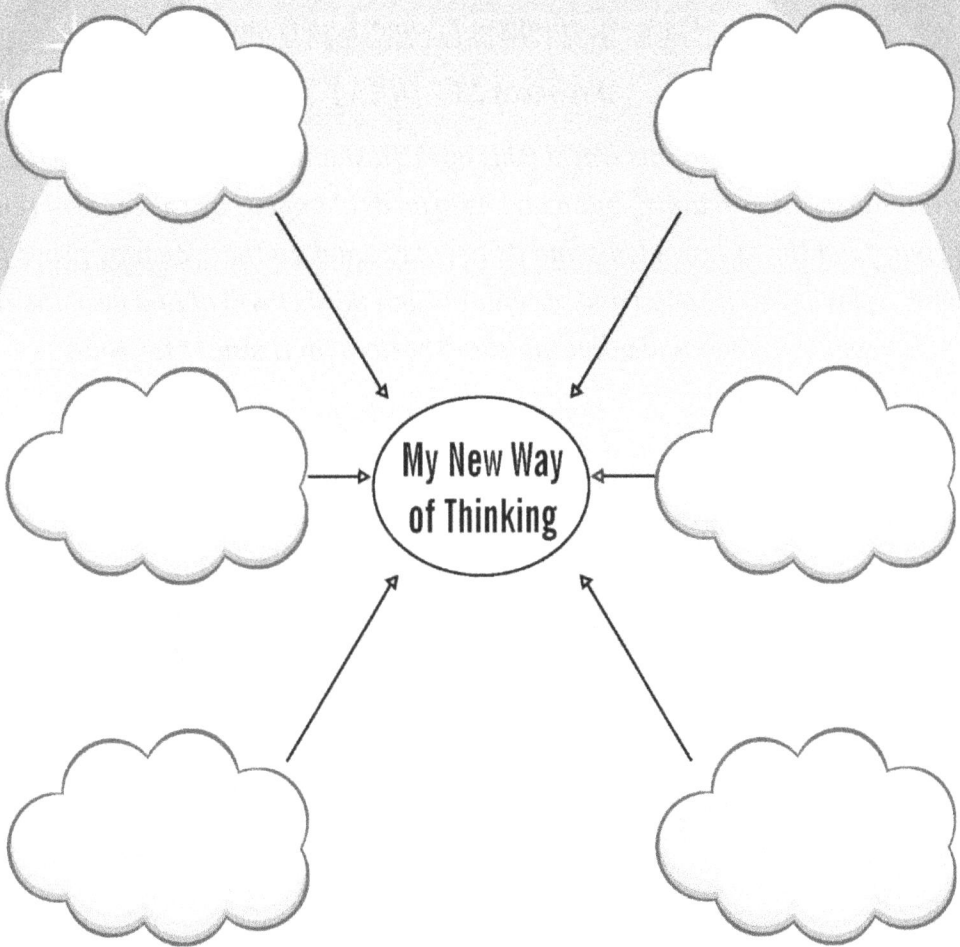

My New Way
of Thinking

SCRIPTURES

For as he thinks in his heart, so is he.

Proverbs 23:7 (NKJV)

Do not be conformed to this world (this age), [fashioned after and adapted to its external superficial customs], but be transformed (changed) by the [entire] renewal of your mind [by its new ideals and its new attitude], so that you may prove [for yourselves] what is the good and acceptable and perfect will of God even the thing which is good and acceptable and perfect [in His sight for you].

Romans 12:2 (AMPC)

Casting down imaginations, and every high thing that exalteth itself against the knowledge of God, and bringing into captivity every thought to the obedience of Christ;

2 Corinthians 10:5 (KJV)

INSPIRATIONAL QUOTES

"The only way you can sustain a permanent change is to create a new way of thinking, acting, and being."

__Jennifer Hudson

"Your life today is a result of your thinking yesterday."

__John Maxwell

"In order to grow we must be open to new ideas...new ways of doing things...new ways of thinking."

__George Raveling

"You must learn a new way to think before you can master a new way to be."

__ Marianne Williamson

"Humanity is going to need a substantially new way of thinking if it is to survive."

__Albert Einstein

LESSON 8

NEVER GIVE UP ON YOUR DREAMS

LESSON SUMMARY

Don't give up on you dream. The following are situations that can cause individuals to give up on their dreams: Doubt, disappointments, setbacks, tragedies, adversity, and numerous trials. God uses people who are yielded to Him. God does not use you when you feel you're prepared. God is looking for availability.

Recapture the dream you have abandoned. Once again, claim your dream as your own. The most difficult time of any journey is when you are in the middle. When you are in the middle, you are too far in to turn back and you are too far from the end to see your destination.

If you are going to achieve your goals, dreams, and reach your highest potential, you must make up your mind that you are in it for the long haul. You must also be determined and push through setbacks.

Success is a process so be patient with yourself and with others. When you are on the road to success, you must learn success lessons such as, patience, perseverance, faith, and persistence.

STUDY QUESTIONS

1. What can cause individuals to give up on their dreams?

_____

_____

2. When does God use people?

_____

_____

3. What is the most difficult time of any journey?

_____

_____

4. In order to achieve your goals, dreams, and reach your highest potential, what are three things you must do?

_____

_____

5. Name four success lessons.

_____

_____

_____

_____

DISCUSSION QUESTIONS

1. Have you ever given up on a dream? Why?

   _____

   _____

   _____

2. What would you tell someone you know who was about to give up on his or her dream?

   _____

   _____

   _____

3. If you were working on your dream and you got discouraged, what would you do?

   _____

   _____

   _____

4. Are you determined to reach your goals and are in it for the long haul? Explain why.

   _____

   _____

   _____

5. What are two success lessons you have learned?

   _____

   _____

LIFE APPLICATION

Using the wheel on the following page, on each outer section of the wheel, write eight strategies you can use when you feel discouraged and want to give up on your dream.

"Don't ever give up on your dreams. Throwing in the towel on your dream is the only way you ever truly lose in life! Keep fighting for what you believe in."

- David Mitchell

Keep On Keeping On

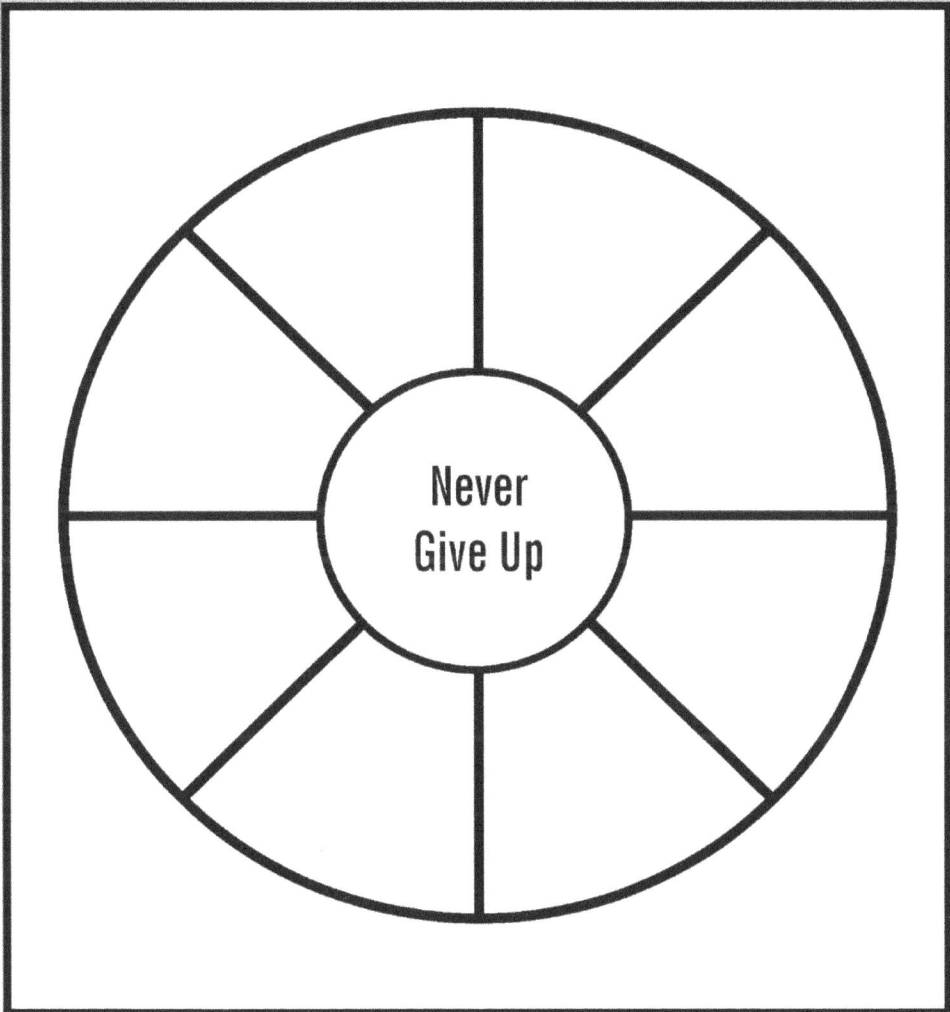

Never
Give Up

SCRIPTURES

But as for you, be strong and do not give up, for your work will be rewarded.

2 Chronicles 15:7 (NIV)

And let us not grow weary of doing good, for in due season we will reap, if we do not give up.

Galatians 6:9 (ESV)

For you have need of steadfast patience and endurance, so that you may perform and fully accomplish the will of God, and thus receive and carry away [and enjoy to the full] what is promised.

Hebrew 10:36 (AMPC)

INSPIRATIONAL QUOTES

"Don't ever give up on your dreams. Throwing in the towel on your dream is the only way you ever truly lose in life! Keep fighting for what you believe in."

__David Mitchell

"Hold fast to your dream, for if dreams die, life is a broken winged bird that cannot fly."

__ Lanston Hughes

NOTES

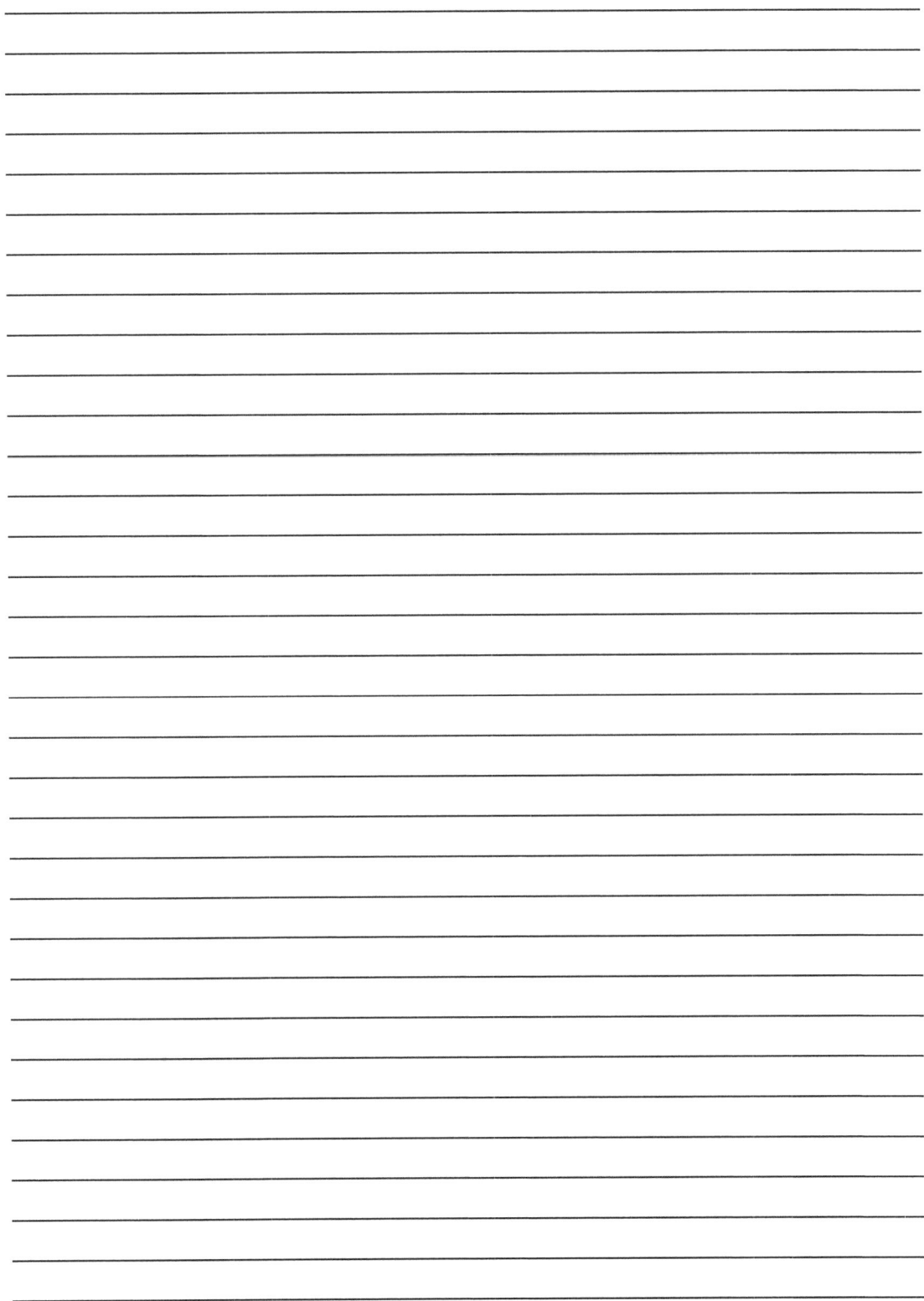

PRAYER FOR A RELATIONSHIP WITH JESUS

If you have never accepted Jesus as your personal Savior, you can do so right now.

If you would like to receive Christ by faith, pray this simple prayer:

Dear Lord, I acknowledge that I am a sinner. I believe Jesus died for my sins, and rose again.

I repent of my sins. By faith, I receive the Lord Jesus Christ as my Savior.

I believe right now that the Lord Jesus is my personal Savior, and that all my sins are forgiven through His precious blood.

I thank You, dear Lord, for saving me.

In Jesus' name, Amen.

If you prayed this prayer, God heard you and saved you, I personally want to welcome you to the family of God!

ANSWERS

ANSWER KEY

LESSON 1
THE GOD OF A SECOND CHANCE

1. God is a God of mercy, love, supernatural favor, and grace.
2. You and God are a majority means God is all you need to begin to dream again.
3. Setbacks are life interruptions.
4. Examples of setbacks are divorce, death of a loved one, the loss of a job, a health issue, and a failed business.
5. Job

LESSON 2
DARE TO DREAM AGAIN

1. Adults sometimes lose faith and hope to dream because others don't believe in their dreams or even in them.
2. Faith to believe for and accomplish that dream
3. Life
4. People stop dreaming for the following reasons:
    a. Fear of failure
    b. Fear of success
    c. Staying in the comfort zone
    d. Feeling unworthy of success
    e. Associating with the wrong people
    f. Procrastination
    g. Thinking they are too old
5. The fear of failure is the apprehension that you will never reach your goals.

LESSON 3
NEW BEGINNINGS

1. A new beginning is a time for a fresh start, a chance to do something over, but in a better, more productive way.
2. When we keep holding on to the old, we are not allowing God to bring His plan to pass in our lives.
3. By forgetting the past
4. His anointing will not continue to be on it.
5. God's [tender]compassions

LESSON 4
SMALL BEGINNINGS

1. Despise
2. The word *despise* means dislike, hate, look down on, or undervalue.
3. If we are faithful in small things, God will be able to trust us with bigger ones.
4. Faithful in the *Greek* means to be reliable and trusted. Faithful according to *Webster* means to be loyal, firmly devoted, worthy of trust, or reliable.
5. If we don't take care of what God gives to us, we will lose it.

LESSON 5
PRESSING INTO A NEW BEGINNING

1. We have to let go of what lies behind.
2. The failures of the past
3. What lies behind
4. *Press* means to exert steady force or pressure.
5. Determined

LESSON 6
DON'T GIVE UP

1. Looking back can cause the following problems:
   a. Slow you down in your Christian walk
   b. Hinder your progress when you are working on your dream
   c. Keep you from doing what God is calling you to do
   d. Keep you from reaching your goals and realizing your dreams
   e. Cause you to lose your focus, distract you, and get you off track
2. Let your eyes look directly forward, and your gaze be straight before you.
3. Looking back can be extremely dangerous to a person's success in the following ways:
   a. Hold the person back
   b. Bring defeat
   c. Paralyze a person's actions to affect his or her future
4. When you look back, you see all of your past mistakes, faults, and failures.
5. Miracles

LESSON 7
A NEW WAY OF THINKING

1. Success starts in your mind.
2. Life
3. No

4. The mind must be renewed by the Word of God.
5. Your new way of thinking is "God's Way of Thinking."

LESSON 8
NEVER GIVE UP ON YOUR DREAMS

1. Many individuals give up on their dreams because of the following reasons:
   a. Doubt
   b. Disappointments
   c. Setbacks
   d. Tragedies
   e. Adversity
   f. Numerous Trials
2. God uses people when they are yielded to Him.
3. The most difficult time of any journey is in the middle.
4. In order to achieve your goals, realize your dreams, and reach your highest potential, do the following:
   a. Make up your mind that you are in it for the long haul.
   b. Be determined
   c. Push through setbacks
5. Four success lessons are:
   a. Patience
   b. Perseverance
   c. Faith
   d. Persistence

ABOUT THE AUTHOR

MIRANDA BURNETTE is the president and founder of Miranda Burnette Ministries, Inc. She is a licensed evangelist. She is also the founder of Keys to Success Academy, Inc., a Leadership Bible School where she teaches people how to discover and fulfill their calling, to make their dreams a reality, to be successful in every area of their lives, and to be all God created them to be. The vision of Miranda Burnette Ministries is to educate, equip, and empower others to be successful leaders and reach their full God-given potential.

Miranda is the author of *Success Starts in Your Mind, Dare to Dream and Soar like an Eagle, Leader to Leader, Keys to Living a Fruit-Filled Life,* and *Dare to Dream Again.* She also makes an impact on the lives of others with her teachings on CD. She is the founder and president of I Can Christian Academy, Inc. Miranda and her husband, Morris, lives in Atlanta, Georgia and are the parents of two adult children, Latrelle and Davin.

CONTACT INFORMATION

For more information or to order books contact:

Miranda Burnette Ministries, Inc.
P. O. Box 314
Clarkdale, GA 30111

E-mail:
Miranda@ mirandaburnetteministries.org

Website:
www.mirandaburnetteministries.org

OTHER BOOKS BY MIRANDA BURNETTE

Dare to Dream and Soar Like an Eagle
The Sky is the Limit!

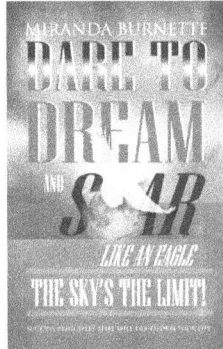

If you are ready to take the challenge to make your dreams a reality, this book is for you. In these pages, Miranda Burnette shares important success principles that will absolutely transform your life. The keys contained in this powerful book will help you soar from level to level in order to fulfill God's purpose for your life.

Dare to Dream and Soar like an Eagle will help you:
- Maximize your potential
- Achieve your goals
- Clarify your vision
- Cultivate inspired ideas
- Release the seeds of greatness that God has placed inside you.
- Recognize that God created you for *SUCCESS*

It doesn't matter who you are or what you are experiencing in your life right now, you have residing within you God-given ability to accomplish more than you could ever imagine. So *Dare to Dream and Soar Like an Eagle! The Sky's the Limit!*

Success Starts In Your Mind
A Manual on How to Think Your Way to Success

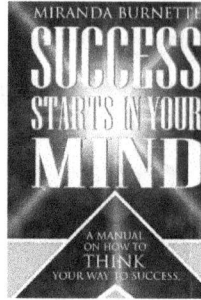

If you could change one thing in your life right now, what would you change? Have you ever considered changing your thoughts? If you are frustrated, discontented, and disappointed with your life, if you want to be successful in different areas of your life, if you want to be freed from the bondage of bad habits, and if you want your life to change, *THIS BOOK IS FOR YOU!*

If you want your life to change, you have to change your thinking. Your life won't change unless your thoughts change. You can change your life by changing your thoughts.

SUCCESS STARTS IN YOUR MIND will help you:

- Understand the power of thoughts
- Develop an understanding of the relationship between success and the mind
- Think positively
- Overcome the fear of success
- Comprehend how what you think about yourself can dramatically affect your level of success
- Realize that *Success Starts In Your Mind*

If you are not successful, or if you are not as successful as you would like to be, it is time for you to start *Thinking Your Way to Success.*

Leader to Leader
Inspiring Words for Women in Leadership

Do you want to be a strong, confident leader? Do you want to learn leadership principles that will take you and your organization to the next level? Do you desire to develop leaders, not just followers? Do you want to learn how to make good decisions? *THEN THIS BOOK IS FOR YOU!*

LEADER TO LEADER will help you to:

- Discover how to be an effective leader

- Develop principles of leadership that will help you be the leader others will follow

- Learn the qualities of a great leader

- Realize that failure is not fatal

- Use your past mistakes as a stepping stone to rise to the next level

- Lead by example

- Develop great leaders

Read, study, and meditate on the leadership principles in this devotional and become the effective leader you've always wanted to be!

Keys to Living a Fruit-Filled Life
Nine Keys That Will Unlock the Door to Success in Your Life

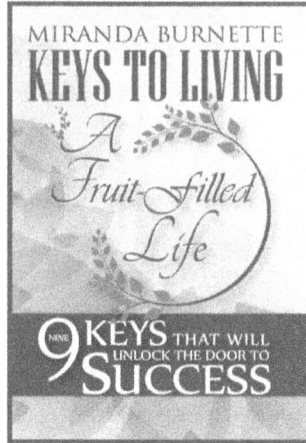

Do you want to have a successful, productive, fulfilling life? Would you like to have a life where you accomplish great things? Have you been desiring a life where you are constantly growing and over flowing with blessings and prosperity? Do you want a life that is producing good fruit? Would you like to live your life in such a way that you make a great difference in the lives of others? Do you want a life that is full of love, joy, peace, patience, kindness, goodness, humility, faithfulness, and self-control? If you answered yes to all of those questions, *THIS BOOK IS FOR YOU!*

Keys to Living a Fruit-Filled Life will teach you:

- How to live a happier more peaceful life
- How to prepare for great opportunities
- Steps to develop the Fruit of the Spirit in your life
- How to develop great relationships
- Nine keys that will unlock the door to success in your life
- How to live the *"Good Life"*

Keys to Living a Fruit-Filled Life will open the door to success in your life and guide you into how to enjoy the abundant life God has for you.

Dare to Dream Again!
It's Never Too Late For a New Beginning

Have you ever dreamed of winning something, being something, or starting something? Maybe you have dreamed of starting your own business, earning a degree, becoming a professional athlete, artist, or musician.

We are born dreamers! When you stop dreaming, it seems as if a part of you is missing. Nothing else seems to fulfill you as much as the desire to realize or accomplish your dream.

God has a specific plan designed for each of our lives. Nevertheless, it is our responsibility to stay on the path to our dream. We must hold on to the dream, cooperate with God, and fulfill the plan He has for our lives. If you have lost sight of your dream, and given up on your dream, it is time to dream again!

As you read this book, it is my sincere prayer that you will pick up the shattered pieces of your dream and rekindle the passion you once had and *Dare to Dream Again!* Once you start dreaming again, this time, don't let anyone or anything stop you from living your dream! Hold on to your dream and don't let it go!

www.ingramcontent.com/pod-product-compliance
Lightning Source LLC
Chambersburg PA
CBHW081516040426
42447CB00013B/3243